T0128924

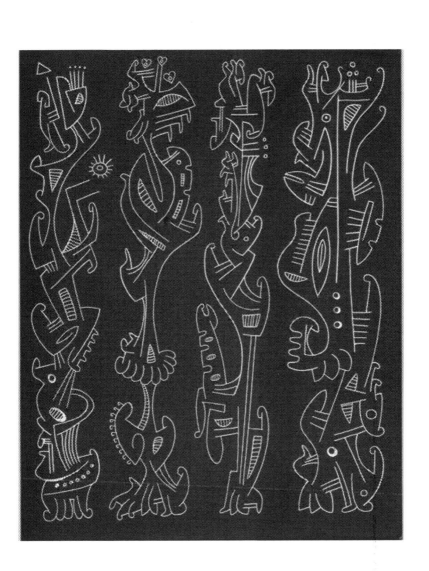

LIVING
LIGHT
LANGUAGE

CREATION SPEAKS . . .

BALA DEVA

iUniverse, Inc.
Bloomington

LIVING LIGHT LANGUAGE
Creation speaks . . .

iUniverse books may be ordered through booksellers or by contacting:

iUniverse
1663 Liberty Drive
Bloomington, IN 47403
www.iuniverse.com
1-800-Authors (1-800-288-4677)

ISBN: 978-1-4759-7995-4 (sc)
ISBN: 978-1-4759-7996-1 (ebk)

Library of Congress Control Number: 2013903926

Printed in the United States of America

iUniverse rev. date: 03/07/2013

TABLE OF CONTENTS

INTRODUCTION

That, which can award liberation from the cycle of repeated birth and death is a great mystery to most materially conditioned souls. The Vedic scriptures of timeless origin disclose the secrets of reviving pure consciousness and coming out of our slumber in 'Maya' to an awakened state of being.

Approaching this subject matter by revealing just what is, 'Living Light Language' can be rather elusive. As it is similar in attempting to describe the 'Tao' which is beyond description and yet with so many words pointing us in a certain direction. It is important that the reader who has some curiosity about the subject matter to utilize their intuitive faculties and discover very practically how this influence penetrates their own lives.

In my world it has been all important as an artist and spiritual aspirant for many years, to discover constantly the hidden symbols and promptings which have led me, finding one clue after another, piecing together the puzzle of the meaning of existence. It adds novelty and mystery and deeper meaning to individual development when we realize that we are in a constant dialogue with our surroundings, meaning life itself.

'Living light language' is the expression of Gods will, being imparted on every level of existence, trickling down, through each dimensional sphere wherein we, pick up the signal and act upon the realization thus imparted.

There is a lot more going on than meets the eye in the cosmic design for us to discover as we choose to consciously evolve in our spiritual journey through this particular life form on a ever ascending path of evolution.

It is from this point of view, that we would like to establish the validity of 'Living Light Language' and its influence in our lives as a vehicle for transcendence . . .

THE YOGI.

CHAPTER 1

CREATION SPEAKS

'Living Light Language' is a term to acknowledge the fact that there is innate intelligence within the very structure of the Quantum Field. That, Source has a master plan, which has been implemented since the dawn of time. The fact that creation speaks to us constantly and we can choose to enter that dialogue anytime is the greatest gift of our Creator. This structured information is a natural control system to regulate every individuals requirements for well being. There is an optimal physiological state, which is achieved through coherence, which is the rhythmic ability of the heart, mind, body to harmonize. Our attunement to achieving this state empowers us to be fully alive and expressive of all wonderful abilities and talents!

Just how, the 'Divine Intelligence' of nature operates with such perfection is what we are exploring. In every sphere of life we are being given guidance for our higher evolutionary good if we are willing to 'heed' such guidance. The mysteries of this creation can be known if our spirit yearns to comprehend such matters.

The characteristic components of 'Living Light Language' that distinguish it from other forms of language is in its ability to upgrade, infuse and inspire one in their continued growth of ever expanding consciousness. Composed of higher frequency vibration, it is a living, consciously active, ever adapting and progressive display of love and light creating an acceleration in individual and planetary evolution. It may assume the form of a written language or appear to us directly as light, sound, or have another visual representation, such as sacred geometry. For example, the Hebrew language is not simply a formation of so many letters arranged to structure words and sentences but is on another level coded with numerical equivalents to each letter as in the sacred structure of the Torah. This Holy text and its 'fire letters' of divine origin, when examined by a super computer analysis, reveals a divine matrix that is veritably an oracle of past, present and future. Such a revelation has been documented in a fascinating book titled the 'God Code'.

Mundane language, or those languages which have developed as adaptations of the root (Mother) languages, are thus, not beneficial in the sense of having any innate capacity to raise ones vibration. However, when any language is utilized to express the glorification of God/Goddess this automatically transmits divine connection and such activity creates a transcendental atmosphere especially when performed in large groups for the benefit of All sentient beings. In this sense, even our mundane languages can be utilized to purify and re-spiritualize the atmosphere, it's a matter of intention.

In a profound work by JJ.Hurtak in his metaphysical masterpiece entitled, 'The Keys of Enoch'. Much is revealed about the composition of 'Light Language' and 5 root languages he suggests are of this origin. Namely the Hebrew, Sanskrit, Chinese, Tibetan, and Egyptian. We can see that each of these written languages are composed of complex characters that have multifarious meanings. These languages and the cultures that evolved around them have been deeply rooted in spiritual concepts and practices. Producing within humanity a desire and quest for enlightenment. Albeit, in unique and culturally variegated ways.

The actual composition of 'Living Light Language' contains within its very structure volumes of information. Delivered through compressed modules of resonate frequency vibration which is accessed through the genetic structure of the individuals who are open to 'receive' these evolutionary messages. A spiritual seeker who has intent to 'download' programs for cultivating higher consciousness will receive on various levels and through various mediums essential etheric information for their continued higher consciousness development.

'Ask and ye shall receive' is the necessary ingredient to properly integrate and interpret the cosmic information one requires for creative expansion.

Terms that help to understand this process by which 'Living Light Language' is received, such as 'seed packets' of information, or 'codes of light', give us a glimpse at the way in which vast amounts of information can be stored in precious phrases, mantras and symbols.

Energy flows constantly from highly refined subtle realms through the astral, etheric, electromagnetic levels and finally into the densest realms of matter.

Everything exists within this energetic continuum. Alternative medicine for example, is being researched with ground breaking discoveries being verified by instruments, which detect subtle energies fields. Most people by now have heard of Kirlian photography which illuminates the auric field of color/light vibration given of by any object within the 3rd dimension. Showing most definitely the correlating color changes to each emotional state or varying levels of life energy radiance.

Bio resonance healing with the use of computer programs known as bio-feedback machines are able to correct chronic conditions that were degenerative by receiving from the body of a client the appropriate 'vibrational information' (Living Light Language) With this information the program then sends electromagnetic oscillations that harmonize and correct disturbed oscillations. Creating an environment of coherent integrated wholeness for the body/mind of the receiver.

This quantum bio-resonance therapy is non-invasive for they allow the body to utilize the appropriate 'information' on a energetic level and convert it into physical healing. One key factor in recovery from any disease is in the level of intent to heal. By affirming a positive outlook and allowing the innate nature of our Heart, Brain, Body system to resonate with coherency thus, diffusing distortion by entraining the energy system of our being with regenerative emotion is all important. In other words, the choice to live according to natural laws and in harmony with our environment naturally provides the appropriate stimulation to lead a progressive life for the ultimate well fare of our body/mind/spirit.

CHAPTER 2

ORIGIN

Some five thousand years ago the Sanskrit language manifested in written form on this planet Earth as the Vedic Scriptures. From where did such a perfectly sophisticated and complete language originate? Sanskrit which is also known as Devi Nagari or 'The language of the Demi-Gods,' emerged from beyond our Earthly planet from the more subtle and refined higher planes of existence. Indeed, it is eternally existent. This perfect spiritual science coming directly from Creator was accessed and downloaded by a pure and great Sage known as Srila Vyasadeva. Referred to as a 'literary incarnation of God,' or in sanskrit terms, a Shaktyavesa Avatar who as an empowered agent was given the responsibility to disseminate this Divine wisdom of the Vedas for the ultimate welfare of the human population.

This all occurred at the close of the last great age and the commencement of our present 'Iron Age' of Kali Yuga. Due to shorter life spans and less memory than previous ages, the Vedas were put into written form for our present degraded human population.

As we research the narrations of creationism from the 'spotless' Purana, 'Srimad Bhagavatam', it is told:

"From the transcendental flute of Bhagavan, 'Sri Krishna' in his own abode, the topmost planet in the spiritual sky, Goloka Vrindavan, came the all enchanting seed/sound of creation which entered through the ear of Lord Brahma (the first created being in this particular material Universe) and entered deeply into his heart. With complete revelation as to how to carry out the act of assembling the material elements, Lord Brahma, after deep meditation on the transcendental sound vibration began his devotional service. (Bhakti Yoga) to the Supreme Person."

A term to be familiarized with at this point is the Sanskrit term, Shabda Brahman. It refers to "the primordial vibration or sacred sound from which this phenomenal universe evolves." It is this, Shabda Brahman which is the very essence of 'Living Light Language'. In its most complete and transcendental state.

Another quote to validate the 'Source' of all creation reads thus.

From Canto 1 verse 1:

"O my Lord, <u>Sri</u> <u>Krishna</u>, son of <u>Vasudeva</u>, O all-pervading Personality of Godhead, I offer my respectful obeisances unto You. I meditate upon Lord <u>Sri</u> <u>Krishna</u> because He is the Absolute Truth and the primeval cause of all causes of the creation, sustenance and destruction of the manifested universes. He is directly and indirectly conscious of all manifestations, and He is independent because there is no other cause beyond Him. It is He only who first imparted the Vedic knowledge unto the heart of Brahmaji, the original living being. By Him even the great sages and demigods are placed into illusion, as one is bewildered by the illusory representations of water seen in fire, or land seen on water. Only because of Him do the material universes, temporarily manifested by the reactions of the three modes of nature, appear factual, although they are unreal. I therefore meditate upon Him, Lord <u>Sri</u> <u>Krishna</u>, who is eternally existent in the transcendental abode, which is forever free from the illusory representations of the material world. I meditate upon Him, for He is the Absolute Truth."

Now, for many this may seem allegorical, mythical etc. however, this vast scope of philosophical wisdom goes on and on to verify the ultimate Truth of this revelation through logic and reasoning to give the most detailed information concerning matters of creation. The point being that creation is directed by personality and functions on every dimensional level according to personality. The so called vacuum only exists as a intermediate zone between the material and spiritual worlds. Let us now continue with the purpose of our revelation.

The Vedic literatures contain directives concerning all aspects of human affairs in terms of four primary areas of evolutionary progress for the individual.

Dharma—Prescribed duty according to ones nature
Artha—Economic development
Kama—Sense gratification
Moksha—Salvation, Liberation

The fifth and most highly prized attainment for any conditioned soul is to achieve 'Prema' or pure 'Love of God'. This is the conclusion of the entire 'Srimad Bhagavatam', which is the condensed essence of all Vedic literatures.

We can understand that all upgrading energies are ultimately for achieving one thing. A complete resurrection of the conditioned souls original pure state of being. A revival of that, individual/blissful nature, which eternally exists in relation to ones Beloved. This SAT CIT ANANDA nature is creators gift to us as we are made in the image of the Godhead. Although proportionately we are minute in comparison with our oceanic source we are ONE in quality with THAT. Being full of eternality (SAT) full of knowledge (CIT) and full of Bliss (ANANDA) is our true nature. However, we have become covered by the influence of 'Maya' or that, which is not. This ignorance of our true nature has been covered by the material energy and we are therefore caught in the hard struggle for material existence. Simply eking out pleasure through exploiting our senses and engulfed in a cycle of painful karmic reaction. This is NOT our native condition. As a fish returned to water reclaims its true environment so we can return to 'Source' through surrender to Divine Reality.

Sanskrit is a perfectly composed and intricate language taking nearly 12 years to master all of the nuances of grammatical usage. It is a language that is sung rather than spoken. This is the native tongue of the residents of the higher heavenly planets of our Universe. It is a celestial language spoken in many different dimensions of Gods kingdom. By grace, we are given exposure to this transcendent scripture. Even though we live in a dense and polluted environment here on this middle planetary system of Earth, there are pure substances which penetrate into this domain for the purification and upliftment of consciousness. As a Mother, nourishes her children, so the Mother tongue of Sanskrit has influenced all of this worlds languages.

The seed mantra of all exhistence which has become popularized in the western wolrd is: OMkara. Commonly known as 'OM' the mantra of all peace. Within its composition are three primary ingredients of creation. AUM, an alternate spelling, refers firstly to the Supreme Father of all Beings-KRISHNA. Secondarily, to the Supreme Mother of all beings—RADHA and lastly to all Beings or 'JIVA' souls. From the very start, this language is giving, in capsulated form, the very essence of the entire creation. All knowledge, wisdom and ultimately pure love of God is accessible through this transcendental literature, particularly under proper guidance of self realized souls or enlightened teachers. Although we, by nature are pure and perfect we have become covered by the three modes of material nature and many previous impressions which cloud our true identity. In the presence of Saints or those who are free of material illusion and full of the Bhava's or spiritual ecstasies of divine union, can in fact infuse us with their purity or suddha sattva quality of transcendental realization.

Ultimately, we want to achieve the effect of 'Transcendence', which is achieved by those who are most sincerely awakening the mood of devotional surrender and service to the Supreme. Coming in contact with fire produces a burning effect. An iron held in the fire becomes red hot and can be used to start other fires. Similarly, by being in contact with the pure vibration of transcendental sound, we immolate and resonate to that frequency thus becoming God like.

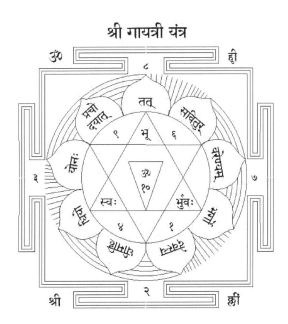

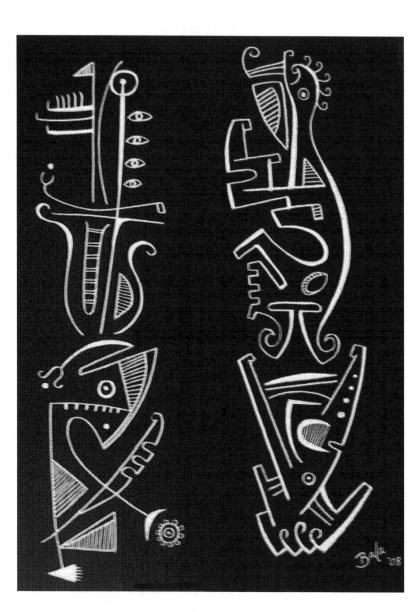

CHAPTER 3

ANCIENT FUTURE

As we pass through the Galactic alignment of Dec. 21, 2012 we find ourselves transfigured as we learn to coordinate within the manifest and unmanifest energy field. Wherein Humankind in its next evolutionary step is co-creating the new vision of life in coherence with the whole.

Passing through a mark in time when dimensional shifting recalls the old world paradigm of solar calendar calculating and its erroneous conditioning of our human society. We will once again be 'free' to exhibit our more full and spontaneous natures in rhythm with the universe and all of life. As individual souls on our continuous journey through dimensions of time and 'out of time', we are discovering the fuller integration of all aspects of our multi-dimensional selves as we become 'homoluminous' light beings.

Through the gradual activation of latent DNA our species is transforming and awakening to higher potential. The most recent assistance in this accelerated process for wide spread activation is the introduction of the 'The Reconnection'. A full spectrum form of energy healing brought through this dimension and propagated widely by Dr. Eric Pearl. The metaphysical workings of this practice are described in the 'Keys of Enoch' as a process of Light work that is connecting the living entity through the Galactic meridian system of the Cosmos through the Axiotonal Field. Just as acupuncture helps to stimulate and energize the energy system of the physical body and optimize the circuitry. This reconnective process acts similarly on a larger scale of mutli-dimensional proportions to re-align all aspects of body, mind and spirit with the greater Cosmic design and correct the dis-connection of our 'old world' malfunctioning.

In unison with this healing modality is the Tachyon discovery and use of Tachyon as a viable emf protector and subtle organizing energy field (SOAF) enhancer. Just as we are within a infinite oceanic field of energy potential spanning creation, the water droplets sprayed off by the ocean waves of this quantum sea are known as Tachyon energy. They seem to have a profound role in the creation and evolution of subatomic particles. Assisting us in attuning to the quantum field itself. Thus, reconnecting with 'Source'. This work is well researched by David Wagner and Gabriel Cousens MD.

As the secrets of the 'Ancients' meet with the co-creative futurists of today our reality begins to reflect the 'Ancient Future' awareness that is glimpsed everywhere in our contemporary society. We see the symbols of 'Light Language' appearing all around us and inside of us! Externally, through the media of TV and movie entertainment as popularized topics with 'supernatural' and 'galactic' concepts has flooded the market. Such as the series 'Stargate' and the movies 'Air Bender' Signs etc . . . Other worldly beings are envisioned to be amongst us as we are 'them' and they are 'us' in a dynamic interplay of evolutionary design. The Maya have the corresponding term 'Inlekesh', meaning, "I am another, yourself." Are we invisioning aspects of our multi-dimensional selves in the grandeur of the ancients as well as the glory of those who seem light years beyond us?

The ancient codes of symbols reflecting the mysterious cultures of the past, be it the Egyptian, Sumerian, Chinese, Hebrew, Tibetan . . . are all embedded into our subconscious, not to mention other dimensional impressions of language and symbols.

India's high art and sophisticated culture has existed through many Great Ages as millions of years of human civilizations have come and gone upon this planet Earth. What we see today of the great megalithic accomplishments of these ancient cultures around the world is only a glimpse of remains of bygone ages. As numerous earth changes continually recycle land and civilizations. The 'grandeur' of our ancestors accomplishments are all a part of continuous cycles of re-occurring themes as cultures rise and fall within the ever cascading sands of time.

Today, in the 21st century with all of our high tech. advancements in electronic devices and digital imaging, we are able to simulate the 'light speed' communication of telepathic reality attained by the yogis. Capturing a glimpse of the frontier of the higher evolution for our species. In our sci-fi dramatizations through movies like 'Avatar' we are able to reflect upon the precious attunement with nature that the shamanic tribes have through their devout inclusion of all of life. While in contrast witness the utterly destructive mentality of conquer and destroy.

We are at a precipice of humanities higher evolution and the moment is NOW to BE the LOVE that We truly Are. For this is the conclusion of all 'Living Light Language' input. Our evolutionary leap at this time is quantum, as the butterfly emerges from the chrysalis we too shall transform if we choose to let go and let God. Being the change we want to see in the world.

CHAPTER 4

DESCENDED KNOWLEDGE

Descended knowledge comes to humanity from the higher planes of existence. Ultimately, from God. This wisdom of creation is made available to those who have the humility to appreciate the intricate beauty and grandeur of the Supreme Artist. With our faulty material sense perception we cannot ascertain the completeness of the mysteries of creation. At best, we speculate and measure with our mathematical devices to probe the fathomless dimensions and postulate a theory. However, this is fraught with misconception. The unadulterated Vedic scriptures when presented in the disciplic line of self realized souls are handed down in complete and timeless fashion for the benefit of all materially conditioned souls. This 'trickle down' effect is the limitless compassion of our Creator upon those who have been averse to divine service by way of a perverted outlook. We assume in our arrogance that we can obtain all knowledge necessary through the ascending process of probing and measuring according to our limited and faulty sense perception. But what we have discovered is the, all to often blunder of speculative hypothesis and theories.

The verifying process of sadhu, shastra, guru is the threefold process by which one uses a check and balance system within the Vedic conception. If all three are in agreement then we have perfect knowledge verified. The Shastra is the Holy Scripture, the Sadhu is the Holy person, the Guru is the enlightened personal guide. When these three concur in philosophical agreement we can be certain of the spiritual truth of a matter. The higher understanding, comes always through descended knowledge. Meaning, that from beyond our range of limited sense perception we can access higher knowledge yet it is delivered unto those of a submissive spirit. 'The meek shall inherit the earth," is a quote in reference to this concept. "Through eyes tinged with the salve of Love" can we see God, is a quote from the Vedas. Thus, through purified senses, having undergone the proper atonements of purification will truly pure and unadulterated wisdom be attained. Therefore, the Holy scriptures and the Enlightened Ones are the mediums by which, 'Light Language' descends into our budding conscious realm and illuminates with the 'torchlight of knowledge' those suffering in the darkness of ignorance.

From the perspective of quantum physics, we now talk about the Quantum or 'Zero point' field. What David Bohm refers to as the Implicate Order or Deepak Chopra calls the Submanifest state of Being. The religions of the ages have termed this all inclusive state, God, Brahman, Allah, the Tao, Great Spirit etc.

This state of 'pure potential' or infinite possibility is indeed the energy of Love and Light emanating as the effulgence from Source. This, All intelligent, Divine Will is a 'pool of infinite desire.' Whereby the observer affects the pool with a ripple of thought (intention) which in turn manifests the creation of the desired object. In other terms, what we think, feel and will becomes our reality!

We are receiving promptings according to the workings of 'Living Light Language' to create according to our higher good. This is really the main point of this book. To enlighten the reader to be able to identify these promptings from 'Spirit' in the form of psychic attunement to the evolutionary patterns of creation. To enter this 'flow' of accelerated life path as a co-creator with cosmic design. Not in aversion to or resistance of, the natural unfolding. It is not by force that we will create according to our greed and lust a society of exploitation. But to the contrary, we shall create for the sake of beauty and harmony a society of respect and honor and devotion to life and the living.

Our alignment must be in allegiance with our Higher Self, the Mighty 'I AM' presence of each individual. With this as a basis, we then align with the 'goal' which is true understanding of our relationship with divinity, the Sweet Absolute. 'I AM One with the 'The Will of God'.

To neglect the promptings of 'Spirit' and ignore the motion in us toward what is good and wholesome we lead a degraded life. Always, at all times there is the promptings of 'Spirit' and through this voice comes the inner knowing to turn towards the 'Light' of being. To participate in awakening with love and gratitude towards our Creator.

'Living Light Language' is the 'music of the spheres', which trickles down into our receptive portals as divine inspiration to create. Throughout nature, on all levels of micro-macro cosmic design is found the divine proportion, Phi. Also known as the 'Golden Mean' 1.618 or the Fibonacci Sequence.

In nature this Fibonacci spiral emerges in the unfolding of all plant life, clouds, shells human proportions etc. In art and nature it sets the standard for beauty. Humans have utilized this proportion in wonderful architectural achievments over the millineums. This sequence reoccurs in our DNA and throughout the solar systems and spiral galaxies . . . thus, we see the divine finger print of God in his very own artworks! A revelation that Fibonacci himself discovered for our benefit by being attuned to the workings of 'Living Light Language'!

It is no wonder now to find that science and religion are merging to become a more holistic world view by which all of life and creation are accepted in a state of Oneness. As the ONE has become many for the sake of interaction and play. Thus, we are simultaneously ONE with, and different from, our Source as individuals with infinite varieties of preferences and distinctions.

Our ascension is in relation to the amount of Grace, which 'descends' into our lives.

This dispensation is occurring in a most profound way at this time in our planetary evolutionary journey, which our 'Mother/Father' God has blessed us with out of limitless compassion for our redemption into the Love/Light of eternity. With utmost gratitude we can accept this blessing and the bigger picture, which it entails!

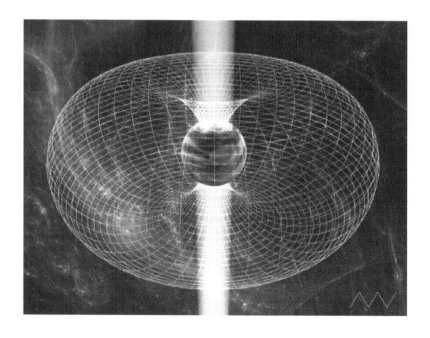

CHAPTER 5

CROP CIRCLES

The modern phenomenon of crop circles that have been catalogued and documented for the last 30 years, leave an indelible impression upon the psyche of humankind. Although most people in the world remain unaware of the significance of these profound and beautiful works of art, there are at least some who can consciously appreciate the communion shared by our Galactic friends. Weather or not everyone is paying attention to such phenomenon, the important work is being done through the implanting of these sacred symbols which are infusing the planetary grid system with it's new alignment. The whole of the planet, including all life forms upon it, are upgraded as we move into 5th dimensional reality and the profound assistance of our Star brothers & sisters plays a crucial role for a more harmonious outcome of global transformation.

It is significant to note, the peaceful nature by which our brother/sister races are choosing to communicate and assist us without interfering in our own choices, yet showing very graphically some guide posts and stimulating references for our progressive evolution.

We can refer to these crop circles as yantras, star seeds, galactic codes etc. The messages are being relayed in perfect 'light language' formula. Utilizing the principle that—'a picture speaks a thousand words' these pictographs carry a vast amount of information that can be imparted through the most simplified format. Encapsulating the appropriate information to be decoded by those willing to receive the message. Those who view these messages in the field, either out of curiosity or intrigue will digest some level of the message on either a conscious or unconscious level which will eventually become integrated by the psyche as a 'knowing'.

The Galactic Federation headed by the Spiritual Hierarchy, which solicits the activities of the starships to deciminate the appropriate 'crop circle' frequency patterns, is described in various books such as the 'Keys of Enoch' by JJ. Hurtak.

The coalition of ascended masters who are attending to universal affairs and keeping a watchful eye upon the evolutionary coarse of our present day humanity. Are truly our 'Big Brothers' in their superhuman ability to assist with our progressive evolution and to assist us in awakening to our mastership. Having successfully passed through the Earth school and working with other planetary systems as well, these Masters of Love/Light, work tirelessly in harmony under divine direction and in conjunction with angelic forces throughout creation to facilitate the unfoldment of higher design.

Communication in the higher dimensions takes place often by way of the psychic transference of symbols and images. Which allows for a much greater comprehension of ideas to be expressed with much less effort than the spoken languages of Earth for example. Thus, 'Living Light Language' is being gradually re-introduced into human society to assist us in this transition into our 'Light Bodies'. The intelligence of our very DNA is being communicated with and transmuted by the incoming frequencies which are all part of an evolutionary acceleration as we are birthed into new dimensions.

Many persons awakening at this time are calling upon and receiving the assistance of 'Angels of Light' whom are their guides and higher selves, being consciously re-connected. This 'reconnection' is the link to super human wonders and the more conscious directive of higher intelligence necessary for an enlightened humanity. We recommend this activity of communion and prayer with the higher spheres of knowing as they are always available and eager to assist one in the process of evolutionary awakening.

Various artist of extraordinary talent have flooded the market place with images of the New Age. The vivid colors, and exceptional beauty of fairy tale creatures and ascended masters are all appearing through the vail at this time, to guide and inspire the human spirit to rise out of the ashes of a diseased condition and heal themselves and the earth. This is being done. We also see that many are accessing and transmitting variations of 'Light Language' as individual expression, weather spoken in 'tongues' or as script. Such 'Galactic Signatures' and angelic channelings will be explored herein.

Within natural order is the sub structure of what we call—Sacred Geometry. Images we are familiar with such as the flower of life, indicate the interconnectedness of all things in our experience. Mathematical formulas have divine origin as the building blocks of matter. We can understand this through the formation of the five platonic solids which combine in infinite ways to create form. The infinite patterning of fractal design is a beautiful discovery of the holographic perfection that exists in reality. As one portion of something includes the totality of that thing. Thus, to give respect and love to a part, includes the whole!

Ultimately, there is an energetic source that stimulates this creation. This building block of all of material existence is the 'adamantine' particle otherwise known as the 'God Particle'. This is the element of Love which binds all things as the presence of Supersoul. Thus, there is Divine Intelligence imbedded within the very structure of all things. As the 'flower of life' illustrates harmonic patterning in this unity of form. Sacred Geometry weaves together the tapestry of the material creation which has its origin in the spiritual creation. Like the reflection in a mirror. Our so called 'reality' is a perverted reflection of the perfect blue print of ultimate, 'REALITY'. Thus from perfection comes imperfection.

Yantras and mantras are the eastern way of exhibiting this spiritual science in a working fashion. Mystic yogis through the ages have conducted the human experiment with great success in performing ritual and concentrated practice for achieving various results through such meditation. The Yantra is a diagram composed of various sacred geometrical arrangements with appropriate colors combined with 'mudras' of hand symbols and uttering the sacred sound vibration of mantras. Just as a science experiment will have successful results if followed with specific and precise methods. Similarly, these tried and proven methods of penetrating the ethers to align with and activate higher dimensional forces will show results upon the psyche of the individual.

Through scientific study we see the evidence of sound vibration creating the resonance patterns which stimulate the formation of sacred geometrical shapes to emerge. Weather this is done in water, sand, with light etc. we have seen various mediums which are conducive to emulating these patterns. Of course, the wonderful studies by Dr. Emoto in his groundbreaking work with 'Miracle Water' have brought to light the full implications of our emotions and their far reaching effects. With positive intent we can transform our bodies, minds and our environment for the better. We have the power to invoke the 'Lords of Light' into our energy field to assist us in the matter of transformation from dense matter bodies to bodies of Light.

We find ourselves amidst a world of various vibrations, which can often be disturbing to our overall sense of well being. It is imperative then to create with intention an alignment with higher self and to follow the guidance towards a life of peaceful, balanced, vibrationally uplifting engagement. Our very DNA is being activated by the metamorphing torsion wave energy (Love vibration). Which is being greatly amplified during this 'Golden Age'. A conscious way to align with this energy shift in a powerful and holistic way is to declare through the mighty 'I AM' presence, that; "I AM one with all aspects of my multidimensional self, my Mother/Father God and the master that I AM." "I AM infinite Love and Gratitude" These spoken verbal intentions are re-aligning ourselves with the Higher Self and our true nature.

The visual impact of regular viewing of these sacred images such as crop circles are gifts from other space cultures for this purpose of integration of our multidimensional selves. To create a platform of synthesis between the worlds as we choose to resonate with the infinite harmony of all of life.

CHAPTER 6

GALACTIC ART

As we view the indoctrinated perspective of art from the so-called beginning of humanity, we see the gradual development of style from the cave mans neo-lithic stick figures up to our present Westernized view of artistic expression. Such art had been a gradual attempt at capturing a more or less realistic rendering of the third dimensional plane up until the 20th century. A collective shift was taking place with the fractioning of the ordinary world view as cubism, surrealism, abstract expressionism etc. exposed another vision of the illusory world. With our more current concepts of quantum physics and digital capability we are now expressing the expanded view of a multi-dimensional 'Reality'.

This is where we will begin our exploration of the matrix of sacred art, etheric or new age art, galactic art or often known as Visionary art.

Sacred Art is timeless. From the origins of creation, All is a play of artistic expression. How can LOVE create anything other than Beauty? Thus, what we see throughout the material creation is a phantasmagoria of infinite design. From star systems to individual planets including every species of life we know. All of the 'Creators' expression is exquisite with texture, aroma etc. truly a matchless gift of ever changing variety, from one lit atmosphere to the next, one diverse ecosystem to the next, ad infinitum . . .

Human beings have explored various dimensions of consciousness since the beginning of time. The 'seers' have documented their discoveries in the form of mandalas, yantras, mantras etc. In the western world we use the term sacred geometry to understand the basic building blocks of creation. The magical potency of such divine shapes lies within this harmonic structuring.

If we accept sound as a first cause, we then perceive that color and form follow. Harmonic resonance results in the orchestrating of the 'music of the spheres'.

As we attune our body/mind/spirit systems through proper nutrition, exercise and spiritual practice we become receptive vehicles for this harmonic resonance to upgrade our current condition and transmute on a cellular level all aspects of our being. The finer melodies of artistic expression can then be channeled by proper vessels into this plane of existence.

Galactic art is one expression of a higher dimensional representation of what we term, Light Language. It is light and information which infuses the living entity with coded language from other realms to be integrated and translated at the appropriate time. Such communication is accessible on a conscious level by those who choose to participate in the evolutionary process. On the unconscious level everyone is receiving these mysteries of communication from beyond which after some period of gestation become realized. Weather a person acts on the information or not is a matter of choice.

The artistic vision which unfolds can run the spectrum from realistic to abstract. The factor determining if something has the quality of 'Living Light Language' within it, is the power of activating and stimulating an evolutionary impulse into the recipient. The infusion of love and light which illuminates the light body into spiritual excitement is a gift of descending knowledge. As above, so below is the maxim which illustrates that our shadow world of temporality is a perverted reflection of a pure and perfect world of eternality and bliss. Divine intelligence is disseminating the messages of perfection as we become more receptive to the impulses. To co-create in harmony with divine order, to express beauty in her limitless grandeur by stimulating the understanding of living from the Heart of exhistence, is our birth right and souls evolution.

The creation of a 'Galactic Art' which reveals the deeper mysteries of multi-dimensional consciousness and how we can easily access these different dimensions through various sacred acts is to be explored. With an invocation of the higher self and the ascended master consciousness we can participate on levels of accelerated learning. Whereby we are taught and teaching simultaneously in the spontaneity of the moment. A channeled expression of our higher self is witnessed and thereby we step into that state of higher vibrational being. To own the presence of 'THAT' which is a more refined aspect of who we are.

These windows of perception are all incrementally important as we, as a species, are taking this next evolutionary step, transforming into a more awakened humanity.

If we look into the annals of human history on this planet (there are other humans on other planets by the way!) we find reoccurring themes of 'Divine Intervention' or higher level input that seems to accellerate the evolution of the given peoples of that time. Weather we are referring to the Mesopotamians of ancient Ur or the Rise of the megalithic Egyptian culture. Whether Atlantis or out of the jungles of South America the ziggaraut culture of the Mayans. A common thread seems to be that out of some basic gathering of humans came a surge of wisdom and creativity that catapulted these cultures into a Galactic awareness which allowed the Shamans/ leaders/ artists to communicate on much higher levels with the cosmos through the telepathic and higher dimensional pathways of multidimensional awareness. Such perceptions may have come through the honoring of the sacred medicines found in these natural habitats and in some cases by austerity and sheer dedication to commune with Source. Whichever the case, a communion has taken place which has given access to the sacred 'Truths' of a greater reality. Thus, the expression of a more profound beauty, through the human spirit in cultural arts, architecture, ritual, mathematics, mystical science, writing etc. has occurred.

The WAY, by which, this infusion takes place is what we are talking about when we refer to 'Light Language' or 'Galactic Codes'. Individuals and groups of humanity are downloading cosmic dispensations at various times on this planet via the Spiritual Higherarchy and the Light ships which are governed by them. These infusions of higher knowledge are made accessible to those individuals who are most receptive to the messages which are permeating the etheric regions. When such individuals penetrate the grosser layers of consciousness and access these more subtle layers, so much vital information is available for evolutionary means. Inventions of all sorts become manifest and people inspired with such vision become catalysts for change.

Even though the terms 'Light Language' and 'Galactic Codes' are synonomous, there is a distinction in that 'Light Language' refers to the purest forms of Divine revelation, whereas, 'Galactic Codes' are delivered as information pertaining to interplanetary communication.

In my personal exploration of receiving and working with 'Galactic Glyphs' I have enjoyed the freedom of letting go to 'allow' these formations to manifest themselves and reveal their story to me. There has been a refining and co-creative element of discovery as to how and best render these images into our plane of understanding. Of course this is a unending process of self discovery. These totemic and hieroglyphic forms have a certain playful, whimsical nature as they reflect various cultural styles. Open interpretation is important in the decoding of various images as they contain something unique for the individual observing them. I may have my conception of the 'inner meaning' of a particular piece, yet, each individual will derive what is necessary for themselves.

These 'Galactic Glyphs' are telling a story of an Ancient Future. Imparting messages through the subconscious mind that will rise to the conscious level through integration. The great mystery becomes revealed gradually, as we go deeper in our personal exploration and longing to know. I will mention the work of Bryan de Flores who has produced a great number of stunning artworks channeled through his higher self that he has termed, 'accellerators'. This body of work is a beautiful example of 'angelic'/higher dimensional art that imparts a message and frequency that can be tangibly discerned. These 'new' forms and images are signaling communication to our DNA strands and activating the accelerated evolution in our body/minds. I encouraging anyone to play with the symbols and images of their own making in a process of self discovery!

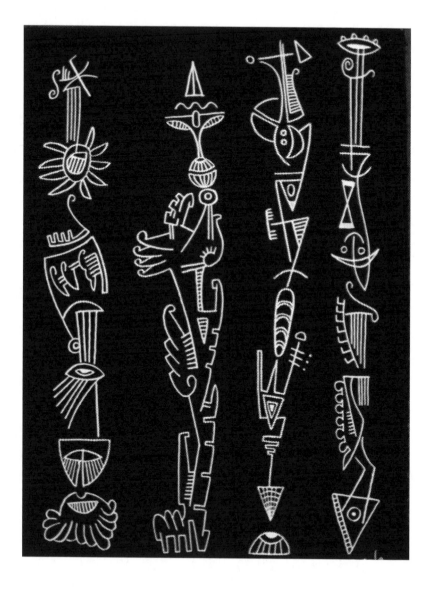

CHAPTER 7

SACRED SOUND

The term, 'Sadhu Bhasya' in Sanskrit refers to the words, which emanate from the mouth of the Sadhu or self realized saintly person. These words are 'transcendental' sound vibration, which means that they are of a purely spiritual quality. The Sadhus are in constant communion with the world of Spirit as via mediums between the worlds. Weather their words are spoken or written the effect is that a conditioned soul, like you and me, can derive the utmost benefit from coming into contact with such divine instruction. Our own innate knowing and pure identity as a soul becomes awakened and illuminated by such pure sound vibration. Sound is primordial, it is recognized as the first element of creation. "There was the WORD and the word was GOD." Therefore, oral reception from the right source is so vitally important in a progressive spiritual life.

We see, that through the subtle vibration of sound, form is generated. The scientific study of this phenomenon is called Cymatics. Of course, along with the formation of sound patterns comes the generation of various color tones. Thus, sound, color and form influence the moods and emotional bodies of the living entities. Our very existence is enhanced or hampered by the quality of sound vibration we allow in our environment.

The intelligence, which is programed into 'Light Language' is what distinguishes it as a 'living' medium for delivering higher guidance. We are generally consumed by mundane noise pollution, yet, the spiritual seeker will ascertain and require a higher vibrational source of inspiration to illuminate the life path. 'Living Light Language' is present always to assist in guiding the aspirants direction towards further illumination. Therefore, it mysteriously appears in many forms, both subtle and tangible. In everyday sounds such as the call of birds and the variegated sounds of nature, be it a babbling brook, the ocean waves, the wind in the trees. We all can identify with the soothing effects of these sounds of nature, which carry a transmission through the sacredness of the natural world, which reveals the 'secrets of nature' to the conscientious person. It is witnessed in the lives of the aboriginal peoples who have 'tapped' the hidden language of nature and become 'one with' her rhythms for acquiring supernatural knowledge of how to extract the vital essence of healing balm from her. Through the sciences of Ayurveda, Chinese medicine, and herbalism in general we find the revelations of the secret world of Spirit.

This knowledge then is apparently hidden and yet accessible by those initiates who qualify themselves through submissive inquiry to know the 'Truth'. Such revelations or discoveries of nature can come in the form of dreams, Aha! moments and intuitive awareness. Whether it is in the fields of science, technology, art, biology etc. Every field of human endeavor has its limitless capacity for newer and deeper revelation. The delivery system of this 'higher knowledge' is what we term, 'Living light language.'

Some interesting questions we can pose are; do we as humans just figure things out as we go along without the influence of any 'higher design' or are we apart of something greater unfolding with the coarse of events, which may be divinely inspired?

In this work we are hopefully bringing to light the undeniable reality of just how Divine Will is continually assisting the unfoldment of humanities and creations emergence.

We have verification that sound, color, form, from subtle to grosser elements originates from a perfect SOURCE. Meaning that, if there is something we deem imperfect then we are comparing it to that which must be perfect. With such logic we can conclude that all form originates from a Master blue print. "Made in the image of GOD." It would be absurd to assume that the 'Source' from which all things come is an undifferentiated pool of nothingness. Obviously 'THAT' very 'SOURCE' will be likened unto its creation. The complexity by which all diverse forms co-habitate in a symbiosis and relative harmony is the orchestration of this Divine Intelligence. An intelligence with preferences and aesthetic quality who is the origin of All Beauty. The origin of All Love. The origin of all form. In whom all things rest or find their support and through which, springs eternal relationship.

Nothingness, is not the 'Source' of anything. Only an apparent medium by which, the immaterial becomes material. Such as the observations in quantum physics have revealed. With the influence of a spectator the emenations of particles emerging out of an apparent vacant void tend to react in uncommon ways. This observation with our blunt material senses is only what our limited sense perception will allow us to be aware of in relation to the borderland of the spiritual realm. If the spiritual world chooses to be concealed from the purview of unqualified 'eyes' it certainly has every right to be and every means to be.

Other studies in the field of sound therapy are profoundly shaping the direction of our alternative healing arts. Weather it is with the crystal healing bowls, or toning of the human voice or the vibration of tuning forks or other digital technologies that are producing healing wave patterns for various remedies.

The response is a non-invasive approach to creating a greater sense of wellbeing. This revival of the ancient mystery schools of wisdom is bringing into our 'New Age' paradigm the more holistic methods of bringing balance to a rather disturbed condition of our sound polluted modern society.

Fortunately, transcendental sound does exist and is accessible for the redemption of our souls pure nature to be revived. The Vedas proclaim that through the ear we shall be liberated. The Holy scriptures, the Names of GOD, the words of the Sadhus or saintly persons are the fountainheads of such immortal nectar.

Through the dispensation of Gods mercy in this 'Age' a great benediction has heralded the 'Golden Age' of illumination for All. The Divine Avatar, Sri Chaitanya Mahaprabhu who is non other than the Divine Couple Sri Sri Radha Krishna (Our Mother/Father God) combined in one form has appeared along with his transcendental associates from the Supreme Abode, to dance upon the firmament of this planet and distribute what no other incarnation has so freely given before. The most sublime and radiant mellow of pure Love of God, Krishna Prema through the congregational chanting of the Holy Names of God. Pure transcendental sound vibration personified!

In all Holy books through the ages there is general guidance towards belief and faith in the grandeur of God and a return to that Kingdom in the spiritual world as the goal of life. What can be found in the literature of the Vedas, which are presented even today in their purity of form through the proper disciplic channels. Is a most scientific description in complete detail of the functioning of the greater cosmic design including a 'road map' for access into the spiritual domain. "Such literatures are heard sung and excepted by purified men who are thoroughly honest" is a quote from the 'Srimad Bhagavatam' which is the summon bonum of All Transcendental literatures. For in its very pages are the unlimited glories of the Supreme Absolute Truth, Sri Krishna. The personality behind the designation of the post

'GOD'. Devotional service, which is the eternal function of the soul in relationship to the lord of the heart is executed under the guidance of the Pure devotee. It is the means by which the conditioned souls of this world are given entrance to the Supreme abode, upon which having entered one never returns to this material world.

In essence, the 'light language' of the 'gods' informs us of this goal. It behooves each of us to listen with attentive ears to the message of God. "If any man has ears to hear, let him hear." As Master Jesus quotes many times.

The message of LOVE comes from the source of LOVE. Through the ear into the heart, mind and soul.

Image formed of holy name "Rādhā"
in Deva-nagari script

CHAPTER 8

ASCENSION

As eternal, blissful (jiva) souls awakening from the slumber of matter, we are recognizing the limitations we have accepted out of gross ignorance. As the vail of separateness is being lifted we are being exposed to the 'Light of a brighter Day.' Which is revealing to us the potential of higher stage development within the human design. This conscious activation of our DNA blueprint is allowing through intention and WILL continued expansion and growth as the butterfly emerges from the terrestrial life of the catipillar.

The option of choice is given to the living entities as 'free will'. The mis-use of this comes into play when instead of choosing divine union through loving service with our Source, we have adopted a desire to exploit and attempt to enjoy separately from our Creator. In this decision we have accepted a bad bargain. For the end result is the accumulation of karma, which has bound us to the endless cycle of birth and death in all species of life forms.

We have another alternative, which is the path of liberation. Freeing oneself from perpetual bondage. To freely, navigate the course of continued evolution through spiritual practice and mastership. Choosing the innate godly qualities of our personality to predominate. To cultivate the 'true' desire of the spirit soul, which is expressed as boundless Love. Thus we reclaim our natural divinity.

Through willingness to undergo this transformative process and upgrade into the higher dimensions of existence we must pass through various levels of conscious evolution. To ultimately reach a state of true and permanent 'Transcendence' is yet, another thing altogether. Yet, our gradual unfoldment into higher spheres is a progressive march in this direction.

As many are well aware, our whole paradigm shift this new millennium is a result of the 'shift of ages' out of the patriarchal domination of the Piscean age into a cooperative, sharing, nurturing age of Aquarius. Approaching the end of the Mayan calendar by Dec. 21, 2012 is a doorway into our newly created 'reality'.

The transformation of consciousness at this time is a crucial response to rectifying a spiritual culture from the ashes of a self destructive course. Our hope, faith and inspiration comes on the wings of the saviours. Those great personalities in the course of history who have risen above the dualities of material nature to teach a better way. Out of causeless compassion such beings have appeared in every culture in every type of body and will continue to come to liberate those willing participants who are ready to embrace eternal life. When the divine spark within is recognized and cultivated to it's highest potential this level of compassion is honoring the sacredness of all life.

Our ascension will move us into the timeless multi-dimensional reality according to our commitment to advance in our spiritual awakening. From budding, to blossoming to fully blossomed consciousness. The world of exploitation that we have known for so long must become a thing of the past as we are accelerated into the 'Land of Love.'

Much is being stripped away from us that has enslaved us in the 'I' and 'Mine' mentality of possessiveness. We are all undergoing the hard lessons of detachment and forgiveness, to become qualified through humility to enter the pure land. To make ourselves anew, in the 'Light of the Living God.' Such a clarion call is being heard as the angels of light stream forth to assist us in this great resurrection.

As purification results and divine intelligence is adopted by us, we become instruments of the 'Divine Will'. Thus, we see that within our midst are the inspired creatives of a new world and a renewed expression of Spirit that will guide humanity. Such an enlightened state is our birthright and truly pleasing to creator, Mother/Father God as we return to that exalted and pure state.

Surrender is the motto of this age . . . As we are aligned with 'Spirit' in acting for the welfare of All. And So Be It and So It IS.

The impact of the 'Transcendental' message is measured by it's transformative effect. Often, we are not fully conscious of the upgrades in consciousness we are recieving as these messages are working their magic from subtle to more gross affects within our etheric field and gradually throughout the body physical.

The chanting of the 'sacred mantras' for example, are divinely inspired seed packets of information designed of perfectly arranged syllables that create the resonation of sacred geometry which infuses the body temple with its presence. This, in essence, is the power and effect of 'Living Light Language', to wholly alter our consciousness from the mundane platform to the spiritual platform.

Multi-dimensional reality is so very vast that an over-all map of the terrain is necessary in deciding where to go and what our options are. This is also provided in great detail from the higher dimensional and timeless scriptures of the Vedas.

Having a complete picture of our limitless possibilities we can then be informed travelers. Not, haphazardly winding up in any old place and wandering aimlessly through the dark of material existence. A torch bearer, a guide, an illuminated master is essential in discovering the direct route to our ultimate destination. Without such guidance there can be much distraction and error. Therefor, a sincere and humble approach to being guided by grace into the land of Love is essential.

We will find that our unique individual natures and god given talents can all be utilized to the greatest degree through such a process of divine service. The Vedic conclusion is in the glorification of the path of 'Bhakti Yoga' or the Yoga of Devotion. Which re-establishes the living entity in ones constitutional position as an eternal loving relationship directly expressed in company of our Mother/Father God and the eternal residents of that land.

This is the sum and substance of ascension to its utmost degree.

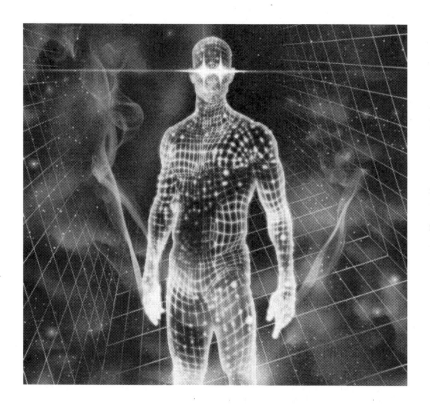

CHAPTER 9

THE 'THE GOLDEN AGE'

In this current age of Kali Yuga, also known as the Iron Age, a time of hypocrisy and degradation, there has come a great boon. It has occurred with the appearance of the hidden Avatar—Sri Chaitanya Mahaprabhu. Who is none other than our Mother/Father God (Radha & Krishna) united in one form! To teach the principles of devotional service and revel in the intoxication of divine love. This Avatar is hidden in the sense that he does not proclaim to be God, but rather to set the example as a perfected devotee of God.

Throughout the Vedas, and particularly in the essence of all the Vedas known as the 'Srimad Bhagavatam. It is described that, the primary incarnations of God descend to this world to reclaim the conditioned souls and to deliver the message of 'Dharma' or (being engaged according to ones nature.) There is very specific information regarding the place of descent, the parentage, the name and form of the Avatars which are described. However, in this Kali Yuga, rather than having the advent of Kalki Avatar, (Which is commonly predicted in the scripture) at the end of the cycle of Kali to wash away the burden of the earth, we are receiving the Golden Avatar of Divine love who has appeared just recently in our human history.

Appearing in Sridham Mayapur, West Bengal India, 1486 A.D. He has appeared as the son of Saci Devi and Jaganatha Misra just as the sun appears on the horizon.

This Avatar only appears once out of every 1000 cycles of the ages or (Yuga's). It is a very rare and precious gift to this earth planet at this time that all living beings are benedicted to achieve the highest and most rare form of 'Love of God'. The whole 'New Age' movement is a direct result of this influence!

He is also known as 'Gauranga' or he of 'fair golden limbs'. Who has appeared in this most degraded of the four ages to inaugurate the commencement of the 'Golden Age' or Prema Yuga (Age of Divine Love). Wherein, a re-spiritualized global culture will flourish and the true bliss of the living entities intrinsic nature will manifest!

Such is the prediction of this timeless oracle of past, present and future, known as the Vedic literatures. Though, all of the hymns and numerous mantras throughout the Vedas are for achieving benedictions from either the Demigods or ultimately the Supreme Lord (they certainly have the potency to do so!) There is one, Maha-mantra for this Age which is most recommended. It has been widely distributed by the 'Golden Avatar' himself and successively through his representatives the Saintly Holy Masters or pure devotees, who are appearing to this day in an unbroken line of descent. This mantra is comprised of sixteen syllables and contains 3 Holy names. Thus, the ultimate example of the perfection of what 'Living Light Language' has to offer is fulfilled in this Maha-Mantra.

Hare Krishna Hare Krishna
Krishna Krishna Hare Hare
Hare Rama Hare Rama
Rama Rama Hare Hare

Even though it appears to be simple names repeated. The esoteric understanding is in the 'Transcendental' nature of these names. Hare—invokes the feminine aspect of the Godhead.

Known as Radha. She is the para-shakti or supremely divine energy of God. The masculine feature of Godhead, Krishna simply desires. All desires are fulfilled by the Supreme Goddess Radha. Krishna means the all attractive feature of God and the name Rama means the reservoir of all pleasure.

Because God is absolute, his names are non-different from Him/Her. Meaning that the recitation of these intimate and very personal names of the Supreme Absolute brings one into direct contact with the Supremely Pure Source of all existence. Within these names exists <u>All</u> of the pastimes of the Sweet Absolute. Every activity performed by God/Goddess is present with the Holy utterance of the Divine Names.

Thus, the 'Golden Avatar' Sri Chaitanya Mahaprabhu came to mercifully distribute, very freely these Holy Names. In doing so, the living entities swallowed in the dense ignorance of this age of Kali, will get immediate relief from the pangs of material existence and awaken the dormant 'Love of God' that is their intrinsic nature. This benediction is the boon of the 'Golden Age' we are now apart of.

In conjunction with this revelation are many parallel events that all line up in the orchestration of divine dispensation for the Age. Such as the 2012 Galactic alignment with (Hunab Ku) the Galactic Core. Synchronizing all planetary fields into the next octave of evolutionary development. Along with the culmination of collective energy shifts in global consciousness over many phases of humanities development preparing us for multidimensional integration. The new Heaven and the new Earth are dawning as the Golden Age commences. "Where there is light, there can be no darkness." The rainbow warriors, spiritual tribes are empowered as caretakers in this Aquarian age of sharing and cooperation.

The resurfacing of metaphysical teachings reveal the supernatural potential inherent in all beings and the interconnectedness of all of life. The 'quickening' of humanities evolution as we make the quantum leap from 'homo-sapiens' to 'homo-universalis' is experienced by one and all. God intoxication is our ultimate state of blissful life! The true culture of the soul can be implemented in this age through this congregational glorification of the Holy Names of God/ Goddess.

Thusly, we have an opportunity to receive the 'Living Light Language' directly from Source and re-establish ourselves in proper alignment to the ultimate freedom and expression of a godly life as this Golden Age dawns.

Bio

Bala Deva Das is a practicing bhakti yogi in the tradition of Gaudiya Vaishnavism for the last 20+ yrs. In 2006 he received a Doctor of Divinity through Spiritis Church from Bishop Glenda Green, which facilitates his non-denominational approach to sharing spiritual wisdom.

As a lifelong artist Bala has traveled the world producing his 'Galactic Glyphs' as personalized 'light body' activators. He is currently a certified practitioner of the energy healing modality, 'The Reconnection' where he lives in northern Florida.

His 'Living Light Language' creations can be viewed at www. Galactic Glyphs.com

RESOURCES

Institute of Heart Math. Heartmath.org
The God Code: Gregg Braden
Torah- First five books of Moses
Key of Enoch: Keysofenoch.org
Kirlian Photography: Semyon Davidovich Kirlian
Bio Resonance: bio-resonance.com
Srimad Bhagavatam: vedabase.net/sb/en
Vedic Scriptures: harekrishnatemple.com/chapter14.html

"The Reconnection": thereconnection.com
Tachyon Energy: planet-tachyon.comthe
"The Field"—Lynne McTaggart.com
Fibbonacci Sequence; You Tube: Fibonacci-World's most mysterious
    number
Crop Circles: Crop Circles Revealed: Language of the Light Symbols
Light Body: "What is Lightbody" Tashira Tachi-ren (author)
Dr. Emoto—"Messages in Water"
Galactic Glyphs—Galacticglyphs.com
Nama Sankirtan—Prema Yuga
Ascension: "An ascension handbook" Tony Stubbs

Printed in the United States
By Bookmasters